ERROR OF OUR CLOUDS

MARILYN JAIN

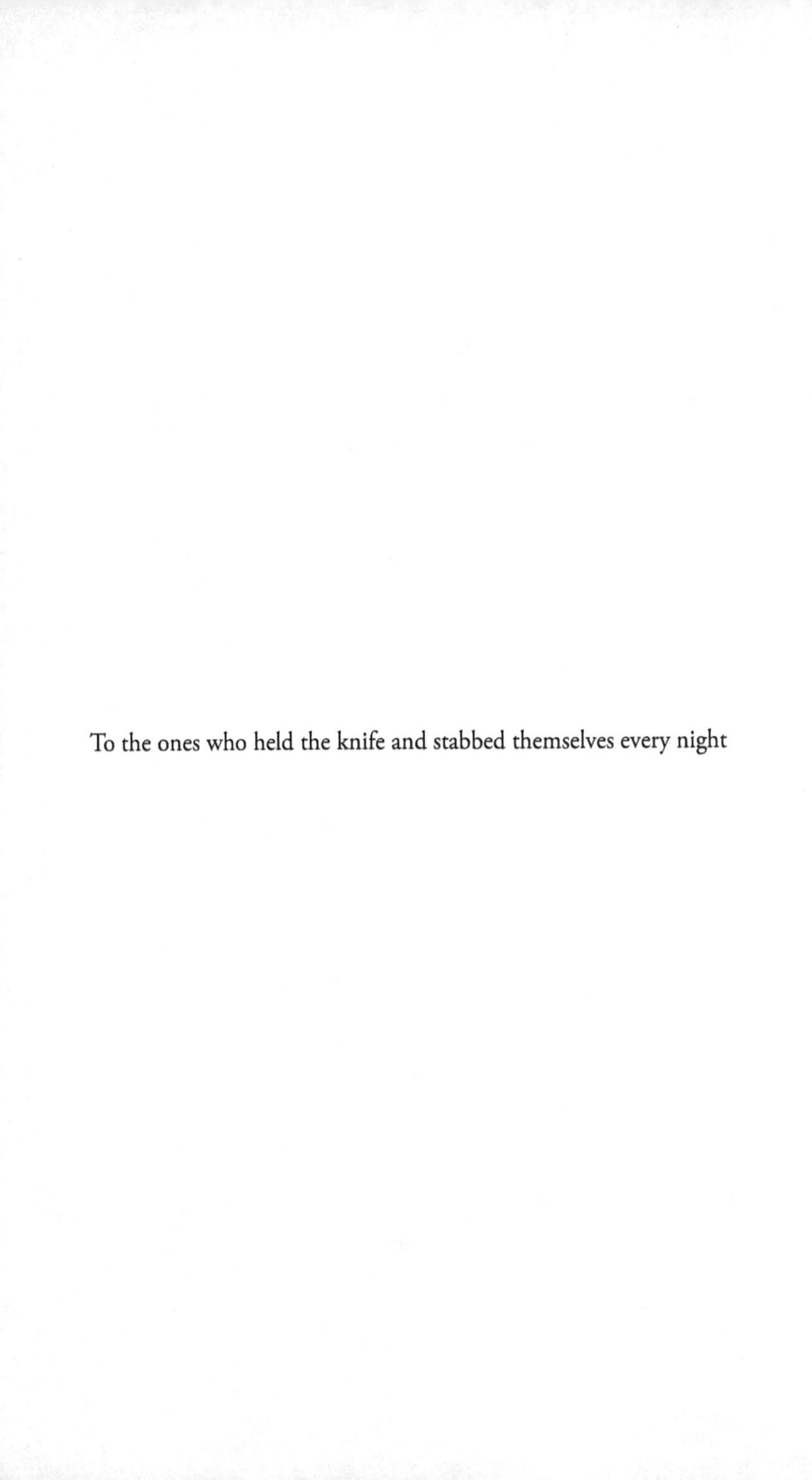

To the ones who held the knife and stabbed themselves every night

Contents

Contents

Contents

Preface

This book Contains a series poems about the truths that never got to live, truths that died inside of me, and the lies I tell the world. Written in those sleepless nights when the world went blind.

1. SAUDADE

First Memory

I dream of my first memory quite often,

A field with yellow grass,

Holding a cup of ice cream,

I look around to see pillars of different kinds.

Some bars of iron painted black,

I wore a pink t-shirt,

With a green mint haze.

This memory terrifies me with the context it holds, I wish it to be

an actual dream

But it's the memory I never wish to see.

Screams of fight,

Begging for mercy,

That place was a horror story.

I looked at the Sun for hours, as it was the only thing visible there.

I saw people in uniforms and grown beards,

I was three at the time.

Trying to figure out what the place might be,

I was trembling by I noises I heard.

May I forget this memory?
It still tortures me.

Why it had to be my first memory.

Home

Been a loner, a soldier, a warrior;
Just for the day when I'll be the one to be saved,
Protected the ones I loved,
But why was it my job to protect myself?

Taking all the pills,
Listening to the stuff that you made mad,
I longed for the day you'll ask me the same.

Made you feel at home,
And remained in the building called house.
Was there for you when you were at your lowest,
But couldn't count on you when I was at the point so close to
taking my own life.

Kill me, burn me alive,
I can't go back to where you left me behind.
I wanna feel at home,
For once in my life,
To know what's it like being cared for,
and not to care.

I wanna feel at home,
And not homesick.

Dear You

The memory of you,

That I never had comes back every night.

To carry me to a world that never had a chance to exist,

I walk there with so much pride.

A world where you hold my hand tight,

And tell me of the world and its cruelty,

A world I'd be happy to live for forever.

Every night I cry for the things that we never got to share,

The bond we never made,

The laughs we never had,

The fight we never fought.

I cry for these things to happen,

Even if they turn out bad.

Some days I miss you more than others,

I go distant from the world to find you,

And say hi!

To sit with you for hours,

And just get to know that touch you have.

I sit in silence to hear your voice.

If the multiverse is real,

I wish to find you in every world.

I sleep every night in the hope I'll see your glimpse,
But how could I even see someone, who I never saw in real life.

I wish you get to see me,
And look how much I have grown,
From day one to the 18th year as you told.

Him

I wanted to meet him,

To see him.

Get to know him,

I wanted to touch that hand, I never had.

I wanted to stare at those eyes, which nourished me.

I wanted to be that kid.

I wish I knew him, I wish...

I want to hug him, I want to be with him,

I wish I knew 'HIM'.

Wait

Why have you never cared for me?

Never asked me where I was,

Or was I fine?

I was living off debts and all you did was rant about your own life,

Why didn't you ask me if I was alright?

Doing things to get you to look at me,

And all you did was taunt me that I am the seeker,

The seeker of attention.

I was a kid!

Trying to understand the world,

You always shut my mouth,

I had questions that still remain unanswered.

I longed for your love, the kind you gave people I was around.

I cried Inside.

I waited a decade for your reaction,

To be loved and cared for.

I took care of you when I was miserable,

Never told you I was sick as you might think I am competing,

I beg you to listen to me.

Always was on alert as I gave you something,
As you'll think I might be trying to kill you.

How could I ever tell you that you are the only thing I ever cared
for.
You are not happy still,
I can see.
Please be someone I want,
I have longed for too long.

Wish I could Tell You

I breathe the pain of your loss,
Curse the moment you were gone,
I wish you could see what happened after that 12 o'clock,

I grew up being silent,
Not knowing you,
Still saw you.

Too afraid to ask questions to the one who feeds me,
I always slept with a conscious mind.
Kids asked me about you, and I always lied,
Till the day truth came out, which I was too afraid for everyone to
find.

I kept a stolen picture of you in my study,
Where no one looked,
Every day I'll look at it and wonder who you were.

To the world I was a silent kid, a dumb one indeed,
But who knew I scribbled those words on the notepad you left for
me.

A person I barely knew, a priestly body, made me think of you
again,
And it was painful.

I cried watching Coco.

That day I was both vulnerable and emotional, for the first time.

The time came when I needed you to be in my life for the first

time,

And you weren't around.

A talk I could have only with you,

A word I could have said to you,

I wasn't able to find you.

Didn't tell anyone,

Went through it alone,

Wishing I had someone to talk to and it would have been you.

I wish I could tell you all things you missed,

From the day you left me behind.

Nightmare

I am a kid and,
My life's a nightmare,
With living ghosts and murderous humans.

I live in the chaos of a weird kind,
Taunting, suffering, and love all in one place,
But if only words were enough to describe it.
This nightmare is a reality I was born with.

They did this chaos so sinfully,
Even Lucifer got insecure.

I live in a mess of emotions and harassment,
Still survive.
Being in fights that aren't mine,
They brought chaos into my room.

I have never experienced peace,
That white dove is all a lie.

Normal

What it is like to be normal?
To be happy on occasions,
To cry when it hurts.
I was a child, who never had a childhood,
I was a teenager who never knew what it is like to be a teen.

Why it hurts, when someone cares,
Why do I cry at happy moments,
My reality is mere stories for people around me,
I was amused.

What it is like to be a child I wonder,
To be free and play endlessly,
To throw tantrums over things.

What it is like to be normal,
To grow being taught,
To have people who baby talk.

Why do I have the wisdom of a 60-year-old,
When kids my age vape around.

What it is like to be normal.

Roses, glitter, champagne;
Girls my age like all things on the rampage.
Shy, sweet, and all girly,
They do things differently.

Maybe it's good that I am different,
From people around.
Maybe I am normal in my own way I wonder,
Maybe I say this to make myself at comfort.

Still,
What it is like to be normal,
I wonder.

Your Name

Looking at the clock,
I talked to you every noon.
After school,
Told you how was it and what happened,
Smiled and went back to work,
I was four.

When I heard the thunderstorms,
I'd cover my ears and say your name,
I told you all the things I kept from the world.

People pray to god, I pray to you.
In the moment of fear or excitement,
All I do is say your name.

But it's an irony that I never really 'say' it,
It feels weird to say it out loud.
A word, that I never had someone to call for,
A word, even a two-year-old is more fluent than me.

I hate people who say it out loud without a fear,
I can't even write it down and make it a poem.

For once, I'd like to write a poem where I can write the 'word'
without any fear,

Your name without a fear.

For once I would like to talk about you without crying.

Just for once,

I beg you to be the one,

I can call out loud.

One More Time

I asked people, where were you?
Were you fine?
They told me not to worry for you as you were in the clouds,
I thought it to be a lie.
You were living somewhere near me,
I felt that.
Even if I didn't know what your presence feels like,
I knew you.

I kept my distance from your memories,
But it always came back.

Now, I have forgotten,
What it feels to be with you,
What do you look like?
It's good that I have,
But somewhere inside me, I want to know you a bit more.

I always thought you'll come back to me,
And say,
'I was playing a game'.
I will get to know you,
I will talk you to,

I want to tell you all the secrets I kept from the world,
I want you to be with me and never leave again.

I have tried everything to forget you,
But my heart aches to think of you dead.

Please come back,
Just for a while,
Be with me as I want to hold you tight,
I wanna be by your side.

I want to put my head on your lap and,
You'll stroke my hair with your fingers one more time.

Please come back as I have missed you.

I want to wake up and see your face,
I'll sing with you and hear that voice.

This world is cruel,
It had made me a dummy of your loss,
I have become strong,
I have crossed all the hurdles,
I have done things that'll make you proud.

I have lived 16 years without you,
Come back, at least in a dream,
So I may see that face one more time.

I have tried hating you,
To make myself stop thinking about you,
But how could I ever stop loving you?

Just once, only once,
I want to meet you and ask all the questions that remain
unanswered.
I want to put my head on your chest and sleep like a baby again.

The world asks me if I remember anything of you,
Never had a word to say,
It was hard to say that you were dead,
I always kept it a secret from people that I met.

I want you,

Please come back as your daughter calls you, Dad.

2. MELANCHOLY

A True Crime

Blurred thoughts and scattered words,

I was writing a book,

I'll never show the world.

A story of a serial killer,

Whose first murder was personal,

Had good choices but always made bad ones.

Was alive but never fine,

A server of justice committed those crimes.

Was a good girl with bloody hands,

Had issues growing up.

Assault, fire, and drugs involved.

Collapsing esophagus and shutting eyes,

I was writing a poem of a different kind,

That talked more than it rhymed.

A poem where the main character didn't have a lead.

High on caffeine and drunk on thoughts,

The poet was a mess,

A product of chaos.

I had people to meet,

Texts to reply,

But s in the corner of my room,

Just wanting to breathe,

And say goodbye.

Dead End

I am not really asleep,
I am just lying like a dead body,
With my eyes closed and my mind running.
Bags under my eyes and tears rolling down my face.
I lie there in the hope this all might pass,
But I am sure this is the 'Dead End'.

A World Full Crimes

Bleeding inside from thoughts of a being,
Suffering for things I didn't ask for.
Caring for things that don't concern me,
They destroyed me.

Living in a world where happiness doesn't exist,
And meteors shower every day.
Where people say the truth to each other faces,
Yet scared to lie.
Smiles are rare to find,
Frowns rule the place.

Smelling like flowers we are corpses,
With filthy truths and a world full of crimes,
Taking in everything we still walk with pride.

We are making a world, destined to fall by our own minds.

Not Again

It's getting dark again,
I was happy before,
What changed, I wonder.

My whole mind turned to a different place,
Like when the Earth goes under eclipse.

That face swelled and eyes cried,
But it wasn't frowning.

I couldn't feel anything,
It was worse this time.
My heart sank,
My insides were crushed,
I feel chaos all over my body.

It's getting dark again,
I can't tell anyone,
As I have tried before,
It's eating me day by day.

I still rot.

Sitting on the floor,
Crying in the basement.

My heart aches with memories of someone,
I never had.
I keep saying the name in my head,
Too afraid to make it echo.

I feel thunder inside my body,
Growling to come out.
I felt pain.

The world around me is all colourful and bright,
Fragrance of petals from a good sight..
But I live in monochrome of ugly thoughts.

I have lost myself again,
It's getting dark again.

A Door To Darkness

Darkness, people say it's place for strong beings,
A place where all the souls of Satan live.
Place where all the wise people used to live, but survived.
I once entered darkness once through a portal of unknown,
First few days were fine.
On the fifth day I met the Monster who ruled the place,
He was broken, way more than I was,
His eyes were filled with blood of sorrow,
Walk of an old man with a young face.

I wonder what broke him but he never speaks.

There I was again, again alone in darkness,
It's quite the place, but it haunts me,
I don't know the way out.

It's not the first time I have been here,
But it's different this time,
Scarier than before,
This time no one was there, just me that lived.

I wish to escape it, just I don't know how,
This place is scary,
More than any Horror story.

It's numb like cold but still alive.

I wish to escape it just if I knew the way,

Just if I knew the way.

Shambles

He lived in barrels of bliss,
Merciful with a lot of pity.
Making a world where emotions ruled and mind tricks faded,
He was an angel with a devil's face.

Innocent, yet witty;
He made people make him tea.

Soon he became Almighty,
Of the treasure of shambles,
A filthy yet prosperous place,
Where only mud had a place to stay,
It was his world of disorder.

Free from crimes and games,
It was heaven in disguise of hell.

Fading Away

She was a saint, with thick hair and bright eyes,
Full of color and broken tears,
She carried the weight of the world with a smile.
She threw away her happiness as soon as it approached her,
She was weird like a moon child.

She hated the ones who loved her,
Envied the one who wanted her to succeed,
She was one of a kind.

Was tired of the world cursing her,
She was numb from all the emotions.
She was distant.

All she ever wondered,
Why she was like this?
She was dead inside.
Crawling for her life,
Made sacrifices no one knew of,
She was a warrior untold.

The word 'why' holds her life,
All she ever wondered,
Why she was like this?

She was bold and fierce,
What made her believe she was a monster?
But was inside her, eating her.

She is fading away,
Away! Into the darkness,
Someone help her!
She is one of a kind.
Making through the world all on her own,
Trying to be perfect.
Help her!
She is fading away…

Life

Wordplay of life,

Impossible to crack,

Sudden feeling of joy taken away by the idea of taking a life that

belongs to me.

Life had different meanings for people,

I have a life too, but meaningless.

Marijuana, Ganja and weed,

All the cannabis filled in this room,

Making an illusion of life that doesn't exist.

This wordplay is hard to define.

To live and let live,

A philosophy indeed,

But what it is to 'live' I ask,

To fade away into time,

Or to make amends for being born?

This subtle art of this life is hard to learn in a lifetime.

Why does a life need meaning,

When the only thing everybody does in a lifetime is to grow, earn,

reproduce and die.

Million questions surround us,

Just to find answers to those already answered.

It's weird to define a life,
When it can be anything one may desire.
This is a wordplay for People with hopes and dreams,
A mere play for those who wish to die.

A Soul Left Behind

A room full of silence,
He lay there on the floor with his eyes open.

Saw everything around him,
As his vision got black by light.
Position of a fetus,
His stomach growls from hunger,
He still lies there with numb feet.

His heart has turned into rocks,
And his mind is burnt.
He lay on the floor of dead butterflies,
Which once got him to cloud 9.

Dirty laundry and open books,
We're on his bed,
With pillows by the side.

He cried without any emotion,
He was just a body.

If sadness could ever have a face,
It would be his.
Cold limbs, tangled hair,
Insects crawling beside him.

He looked in the vacuum,

As he saw memories of her.

He was mediating horror,

He is not where he seems,

He is distant from the world underneath.

The Smell Of Death

With dead flowers in one hand and coffee in another,

I walked to the graveyard.

Moonlit night, a little rain, and wolf's howling,

It was perfect to travel eternity.

2:00 AM in the morning,

All still with a concert of crickets,

Rain and soil,

This is where I could smell *death*.

I sat beside the grave of a loved one,

Wishing them well in hell,

Making Amends.

Walked towards the moon,

To find those lost souls,

Flowers rotting in my hand,

I held them tight.

I heard people talking, I ran from the place.

Moon was close and so were the eyes that sought me.

It was the gate of shambles, where the moon stood waiting to see

me hang this body,

And be with the ones I just met.

Just like the patriot,
I was there with my hands tied and rope around my neck.

I was hanged by the moon that night.

3. EPHEMERAL

A Lost Battle

Standing on the battlefield,
Covered in blood I still walk towards my enemy.
Chariots, horses, elephants;
All racing in my direction,
I hail for my army.
A dusty day with the Sun setting,
I saw slavery in my army's eyes.

An arrow punctured my lung,
I almost fell where my land ended.
They hosted their flag on my chariot,
I lost my mother, my land.

They took me to their kingdom and made me their slave,
I cried blood.

They took what I made mine,
Ruined what I loved.
Tortured my people for money,
My land was in the hands of someone who rules but does not care.
My mother was crying,
But there I lay in the cave of no sunlight,
Praying to die.

Till Eternity Falls Apart

There were two lovers,

Madly in love.

The world hated them for what they had was real,

They had their chaos to fight for what they loved.

Not like other stories,

They became one.

She looked like the moon and he looked like Sun,

They got married on the 31st.

Saying their vows they both cried for love,

They were just like doves.

Pure.

But someone said right,

True love stories don't last for life.

Sun always burned to lit the moon,

But they never were together.

This story lacked a villain.

So destiny took the part,

Made them get on the yacht.

Nature took revenge too, making the yacht flood.

They knew their end was near,

Went to their room and sat on stools.

Holding hands they put their heads together,

And promised,

'We'll find each other again, maybe in another life or in another

world',

'Till eternity falls apart'.

Their bodies lie in graves with statues above,

I hope they found each other again,

In another life or another world.

A Reader

I used to sneak under my blanket with a torch to read A book I
adored for long,
I'll never say I love to read,
But it takes me to a distant place.
A place where the chaos ends,
A place full of hope,
A place I can call mine.

All the fantasies I read,
I traveled to unknown universes.

All the romances I read,
Made me a hopeless romantic.

All the crimes I read made me love murders.

And All those psychological thrillers,
Made me a psychology girl.

All that I have in me is what I got from books.

It's something I started as an escape from reality,
Instead, it became my personality.

I am addicted to books,
Libraries fascinate me,

Smell of new books calls my name.

I have a thousand lives and seen many deaths,
I have created worlds in my mind and destroyed the one I lived in.

I have given my imagination an endless path to travel,
Reading has given me the peace I have longed for forever.

Shiny big eyes,
With the biggest smile,
She walked with pride,
While everybody saw her cry.

Damsel

I remember the kid who used to lock the bathroom door to hide
her tears,
I remember the kid who shoved her fingers in her ears to eliminate
the noises,
She begged to let her keep her childhood but was left unheard.
Now she has become strong, and cold,
Not like she was before.
She has lived through the chaos,
She has made sacrifices,
She is done with the mess, she didn't ask for.

She is Marilyn, not the Damsel, but the Devil
Here to slay.

Why, My Love, Why

You, my love,
Why don't you see yourself the way others do,
Why do you hate your being?
Why do you sabotage yourself?
Why do you think of yourself as worthless?
When everyone tries to be like you?

With a thousand admirers and a million haters,
Why do you still want to sit in your room and sob about things
that didn't happen?
Why can't you be happy for yourself?
Why my dear, why are you like this?

The world sees on the mountaintop,
But you still stand on the ground beneath.

Why don't you feel accomplished?
Why do you do this to yourself?
Why my love, why?

You are everything others want to be,
All the things they can't imagine.
But you think of yourself as a parasite.

Stop doing this to yourself,
You deserve to feel good at moments of your own.
My love, be happy,
You are worth every penny.

Hey! Little Woman

Hey, little woman,
Don't worry, it will get better.
You spotted a change today,
And you should not be ashamed.
People treat you differently for they are not able to understand
you,
You are braver than you think.

Hey, little woman,
This is you from the future.
Don't lose hope!
Don't let people come near you,
You'll shine as the most radiant comet.

Hey! Little woman,
You'll make your mum proud,
You'll do things you're most afraid of.

Hey! Little woman,
You have some hurdles coming up,
They'll shatter you,
And you'll be in pain,
But remember to stay intact.
You'll be left out and always be mocked,

But you'll find a way to shut mouths.

Hey! Little woman,
Don't cry.
It's all supposed to happen,
To make the one and the only kind.
Don't try to find comfort in those who break you.

Hey! Little woman,
Don't worry,
I'll always be there for you.

4. ARCANE

Queen

Was told a million stories of the princesses,
The one with guards and horses.
A prince to protect and always be by her side,
Cinderella, Ariel, Snow White.
All miserable saved by a prince,
Got to be a princess but never a Queen.

Heard a story of a girl with no men around but she got it all under control,
Lived in the cold, so as she became.
Had the power no man held before,
She was the Queen of her own damn World,
Got the army, got the money,
All she earned on her own.
She was built from scratch,
Not a product of sympathy.
She was tough and knew what she had to do.

Queen and princess,
Mere words, but had different meanings.

Out of those million stories,
One got my attention.
One where the abusive King was killed by the Queen,

It was all hers when he robbed her.
She made it hers again,
Even if meant to kill the one she loved.

I am that Queen, was never his princess,
I like naked truths and brutal lies.
I am built like no other,
You may excuse yourself,
As I may pass on to another.

A Girl In Grave

Let's hear a story of a 19-year-old,

Who fell for a boy who wasn't true.

He kept her on leash with fierce eyes and a controlling mind.

She was young,

She was naive,

She fell for a boy who was a lie.

She carried scars for years of disgrace,

She was tough, but still a child.

She was buried under the stars by the boy,

She kept crumbling in the grave of pale lies.

She was a fire but was still sensitive,

She was then, Ruined.

He punished her for the crimes she didn't do,

Let's hear a story of a 19-year-old,

Who fell for a boy who wasn't true.

She held the tears in her eyes,

For the sake that she was right.

She is now in the grave of her love.

Hail! The girl who fell for a boy untrue,

One day, She'll Rise again,
To make Amends to the person who dug her grave.
To Revenge on the one she loved.

She'll rise again,
Again, from her grave.

Last Goodbye

I have mended my thoughts just to be in your control,
I have made my dreams Nightmares to fit in your cruel.
I have left my soul to be in your mind,
I did everything I could to make you happy and proud.

I may be the worst one alive, but certainly not the worst kind.

You made me feel insecure about the things I enjoyed,
You took away my pride, just to fulfill your desire.

I may be the worst one alive, but certainly not the worst kind.

I wrote the poems for the things I couldn't say!
I am not sorry, hence it's the last Goodbye.

Glad We Broke Up

Purple sky of Neverland and silver coins of a fairy tale,
It was all in our hands when met for the last time.
A screw of cocktail and a bottle of guilt,
We carried it with us all this time.
Trying our very best to make it work,
Not because we wanted this,
But we were tired to look for anything new.

Purples were blue and silvers were ashes,
It was a nightmare we portrayed.

At Dawn of February, we said our goodbyes,
And sighed in relief.
We were free.

Good at pretending,
We made it our lives.
I am glad we broke up this time,
Before it took our lives.

Cruel

Dead roses with living butterflies,
Naked truth with brutal lies.

I have fine lines from smiling,
Yet I don't know what a smile feels like,
My eyes have all the wrinkles of joy,
Yet the only thing they ever felt is pain.

Cold heart with blooded hands,
Burnt cigarettes with bouquets.

I may have become cruel but still that old soul with delicate sight,
I have found peace in physical pain and,
Happiness in stars.

I have lived what you hear in crimes,
I have survived what one wishes not to see.

Yes, I have become cruel.

Enough

Could have been the fairy tale you always wanted,

Could have been that innocent fearful girl you wanted,

I wished to be your bride, not your slave,

I wanted the world, you gave me plaque.

I am not the kind of girl you wanted but was a mere dream you

threw away.

Thanks to you I know what pain feels like.

I broke myself first to break you,

Said no to you and killed myself,

I thought I loved you, but that wasn't true.

I wanted to be with someone because I loved them, not because I

feared them.

Here! I hate you and I always have,

Call me toxic because I am.

The World You Promised Me

Seeing you with someone else breaks my heart,
You say things that were once used for me.
You left me one day,
And I lose you every day.

I gave you my heart and you threw it away,
Now that you have found 'the one',
You do things, promised to me.
You kissed them where I kissed you,
Proposed to them on the night you asked me out.
Gave them the ring you bought for me,
Are you really in love, or looking for someone like me?

Gave them the world,
We wished for.
Took them to places,
We wished for,

On this day when you tie your knot,
You are using our safe words as your vows,
You seem happy but I hope they break as you broke me.
I wish you a heartbreak,
The kind you gave me.

Leave!

May I ask something,

Where were you when I had nothing?

You say that you miss me when I have lost myself now,

Why you didn't want me then and why now?

Why you left me in the first place?

Broke me and lost me on eclipse?

I had you then, I don't want you now.

May I ask something,

Were you ever in love with me or you always lied?

Did you leave because of her, or you just wanted to get rid of me?

I miss you too but I don't want to do this shit now,

My heart says go to him,

But my mind won't agree.

Leave me now!

Leave me now!

I scream.

I had you then,

I don't want you now.

I have said this before, and I'll say it again,

Mister, leave as you did the last time,

Made me yours and left me in disgrace.

I told you my secret, I told you about myself!
You used it, you used it against me!
I trusted you but always played.
I think I fell for those brutal lies.

Tried a million times to hate you,
To forget you,

But I could never stop loving you!

You left me then,
I leave you now.
Take my word for forever and ever,
I HATE YOU!
Always and forever.

5. ELYSIAN

A Daydream

I saw you on the day when the Sun looked like fire and the room

smelled like peaches,

You entered the room and took me like a daydream.

I asked you for a dance and you agreed,

All I did through the dance was stare at those marble looking eyes.

Without even bothering what song played that night,

I went home and slept with you on my mind,

And thought about till the next Saturday arrived.

There is something about you so amusing,

That I can't help it.

I hope we meet again someday,

Someday, perhaps the ballroom,

Someday, when the Sun will look like fire and the room will smell

like peaches.

The Corridor

Dreamt of you last night,
In an open corridor with blinding lights,
You were with dandelions.
Walked towards me with a smile,
Held my hand and walked me outside the building,
Just before sunrise.

I woke up, thinking of you,
Met you with a blushing ache face,
And surprisingly you had that too!
We saw that and sat with trembling hands,
I just hoped you had the same dream too.

We ate, we went home,
Thinking of each other.
It was midnight,
I couldn't sleep,
Texted to see if you were awake,
And you were!

We talked for hours and fell asleep on the call,
We dreamt of each other again.
And woke up with a blushing ache face again,
Said hello in the morning,

And smiled through the day,
Hoping it all will happen again,
Someday!

Under The Starlight

It was the night when a star fell off the sky,
It was the time, I knew I have fallen for you,
It was the night I wanted to say 'I love you'.
I saw that in your eyes too, but we were too afraid to do so,
I kept staring at your smile and you looked into my eyes.
That night, the world was dead, nobody mattered.

That night We were in love!

Looking at each other we said nothing, but our eyes did,
I knew you did and you knew I did too.
We went for a walk under those shimmering stars that yelled your
name,
We both took exact turns to find the place where we met the first
time.

You took to the bridge and I held you tight,
Watched that still water with the curiosity of a three year old,
Holding hands, we looked into our eyes.

You bowed to get on your knees and seeing that I did too,
You pulled a tulip and I pulled a rose as you liked.
We had those with us all this time,
Laughed as we saw how our brains work the same.
Our thing was to count till ten and we did,

And said 'I love you' and blushed like a moon child.

That night we fell in love
Under the starlight!

Like You

When I see you my heart skips a beat,
With a sinking heart and brightening eyes,
I think of you every midnight.

You make me feel safe,
I can be a kid around you,
do crazy stuff,
And you join me too!

You are the best thing that happened to me,
You are an angel with no wings.
The sweetest voice with a humbling touch.

You make me feel at home,
When I cry I have you by my side,
I turn to you when things go out of hand.
I want to tell you,
You matter to me and you'll always have me by your side,
Even if destiny takes us apart.

I could never describe how much I love you,
But I can only say that,
I was lucky enough to love someone like you.

A Bit More

You made me mad about you, the way you looked at me every
time I ate,
Gosh! Why didn't I faint?
You have got me hooked,
I can't think of anything but you.
Making it impossible to function,
You've got a rent free place in my mind.

For a hopeless romantic girl, you came out of a novel,
I never thought I'll have this with someone,
But you have got what it took to be mine.

We liked each other,
We had our fights,

We have fallen in love.

I don't what's left,
But it's certainly not us.
I don't want this to ever end.

I wish to stop the time and make this moment last forever,
May we be in love a bit longer.

I have loved your soul and touched your mind,

May we have this for a bit more while.

The Day You Became Mine

Under the stars, on our knees, we said we loved each other for the
very first time.
From that day I fell for you a bit more every day,
Those gossips and library dates, you picked out books for me and I
picked you some comics.
Those escaped parties and mocked people,
You were everything I wished for.
That pretty face and killing smile,
Those marble eyes and rustic hair,
It was like my childhood dream came true,
A prince who rode a horse.

The day you asked me to meet your family,
I was terrified but was happy a bit more.

I know you want to do this so badly, but please give me a chance.

I wanna take you out on a casual date,
A nice dinner, a walk perhaps, then we'll go to our terrace and I'll
pour you some wine,
When you'll take the first sip,
I'll take the ring out and bend on my knees,

And I'll say

"I never thought I'll love someone this hard,
You are my dream, my love,
You have made me mad"

"I wanna go grocery shopping together and,
And fight over whose gonna make the
breakfast.
I wanna lie to you about how you look and,
And tease you for the rest of your life.
I wanna kiss you bye every morning when we both go to work,
I wanna disturb you for the rest of your life"

"I want you to be mine,
For always and forever.
And do you want me to be yours?"

"Will you marry me and stick by my side like an eternal ghost?"

Vows [I]

Seeing you walking down the aisle,
The life I had with you flashed in front of my eyes.
Seeing you in that pretty white dress,
Reminded me of the day when you showed me the dress you wore
as a child.

You asked me to marry you under the starlight,
With roses and wine.
You, my love, are everything I hoped for,

Here we are standing face to face,
Waiting to say vows,
I'll go first this time.

"Without you, I'll be nothing but the dust of Sahara,
Your breath is my song and,
Your smile is my dawn.
I will always protect you and make you breakfast,
Take to watch comets and play like children.
I want my last breath to say your name,
From this day,
I'll never let you cry.

I loved you then, I love you more now!
Honey, make me yours as you're all mine.

Vows [II]

With tears in my eyes,

I heard your vows.

Seeing you waiting for me as I walked down the aisle,

Reminded me of the day when you showed me the dairy you

wrote as a child.

Seeing you in that tux made me fall for you again,

You have said your vows,

Now let me say mine,

"I still remember the day I met you,

The fiery sun and peachy room.

We were damned looking in our eyes.

You complete me as a poem completes a poet,

You are everything, my love.

I want to make you mine,

I'll protect your tears and make you feel at home.

With a newspaper by your side,

I'll make you dinner every night,

With roses and wine.

Take you fishing and eating ham,

Tasting coffee and backpacking around Europe.

We are two people with empty hearts,
Trying to fill the ones we loved.

Will you be mine?
As I am all yours.